by Marilee Robin Burton

illustrated by Cindy Revell

Scott Foresman

Editorial Offices: Glenview, Illinois • New York, New York
Sales Offices: Reading, Massachusetts • Duluth, Georgia
Glenview, Illinois • Carrollton, Texas • Menlo Park, California

A little sunshine came through the small window of Meg's new home. The light was dim in the soddy near the hill. Still Meg knew it was morning. She could hear her mother cooking corn mush. It was time for Meg to get up and get on with her chores. First she had to wake Billy and fold the bedding. Then she had to check the dugout for chicken eggs and fetch water. Then she had to sweep the dirt floor and churn butter.

Life on the prairie was an adventure! But the adventure was hard work. And Meg was homesick. She missed her old friends so much. She missed wearing pretty dresses. She wanted to be back in Boston at Grandma's. Grandma had a big house with a porch and a piano. That was a home!

Meg climbed out of bed and ruffled her
brother's hair.

"Time to get up!" she called.

After a gentle push, Billy rolled off the bed. Meg
folded up the bedding. Now there was more space
inside the sod house. Meg pushed aside the curtain
that hung from the ceiling. She could see her mother
at work in the kitchen corner.

"Why couldn't we stay in Boston with Grandma?" Meg bristled aloud.

She pulled her rough work dress over her head, and then helped Billy with his flour sack shirt.

"Now, Meg," said Ma. "Don't be naughty. This farmland is all ours! Someday it will be worth all the hard work."

"Soon the school will be built and you will make new friends. Now try to be brave. Please!" Ma said.

Meg bristled again. She was trying! Meg tried daily to work hard and be happy!

"Good morning!" Pa called cheerfully. He came in with a bucket of milk. "Everyone to the table now! Time to start the new day!"

After breakfast Pa went quickly back to work. This time Billy went along too. Then Ma heated water to wash dishes. She would use the soap she and Meg had made last week. Meg got out the linen towel to do the drying.

Ma talked to Meg about fixing up the dark room by pasting newspaper to the walls. Meg's mind wandered back to Grandma's pretty house. Grandma's house was a real home. *Thud!* Meg dropped the bowl she was drying.

"MEG! Be more careful. I don't want to have to punish you. We have so much work to get done before the sun goes down. Go check for eggs now. I'll finish drying the dishes."

Meg stepped into the bright sunshine. The sky was clear blue. There was a sweet smell in the air. She headed to the dugout for the eggs. Wildflowers were blooming in its grass roof. "Some things are pretty on the prairie," Meg said with a grin. She opened the door.

Searching through the nests, Meg found seven eggs. She carefully carried them in a straw basket, back to the house. Meg didn't want to drop anything else today!

Then Meg grabbed the water pail. She started toward the stream. She and Pa had set little guideposts along the way. They had tied bits of colored cloth to the posts.

Meg followed the guides all the way down to the stream. At the water's edge she dunked the pail in and filled it. Then she set it down and splashed her face with cool water. Meg began to hum a song. But out of the corner of her eye she saw something move. She turned. There Meg saw a brown rabbit peering right at her.

"It is a nice song, isn't it?" Meg whispered. "My best friend in Boston taught it to me. Do you want to learn it? Would you like to be friends?"

But before Meg had finished talking, the rabbit darted off. Meg grabbed her pail. She scurried after the rabbit. Meg tried not to spill the water as she ran! The rabbit dashed into the tall rushes. Meg was so anxious for a playmate that she followed right after it without thinking.

It was only moments before Meg lost sight of the little rabbit. Still, she hunted in the tall rushes a while longer before giving up. "All right then, don't be friends," Meg said. "It's time for me to go back anyway." She turned around.

"Oh dear," cried Meg. "Which way is back? Every way looks just the same." On all sides there were only rushes. "Ma will think I've been naughty. I hope she won't punish me for taking so long," Meg said.

Meg searched for the cloth guideposts. Soon it
was not punishment she feared! What frightened
Meg now was being lost. She feared never seeing
the soddy again. Meg pictured Billy, Mama, and Pa
sitting round the warm wood stove at night. Tears
wet her cheeks.

"You naughty rabbit! You made me lose my
way!" Meg said aloud to no one. "What shall I do?"

Just then Meg heard Pa's familiar whistle. And there was Pa, striding through the rushes.

"Oh, Pa, I wandered off the path and got lost."

"Yes, we were afraid of that when you were gone so long," said Pa.

In a moment Pa had gathered Meg in his strong arms.

"I just want to go home now," said Meg with tears in her eyes.

"Meg," answered Pa, "you know we cannot go back to Boston."

"No, Pa," said Meg. "I'm talking about our real home—the soddy near the hill."